Xspeirience Art Publishing Presents

The Art, Poems And Thoughts Of A Wrongfully Convicted Father

by

Xspeirience

ACKNOWLEDGMENTS

Mom, I want to thank you for everything you do, and all you have done. I know it's hard on you having a son in prison and not being able to help him the way that you want to. Trust me, I understand. The biggest thing for me to get out of my mind is losing you not being no where around. It kills me to know that life is never promised, to any of us. I wish a lot of times that you could live forever, but that is selfish on my part. I just want you to know how much I appreciate all that you do. I will do all that I can to make it home, but in case I don't, I will make sure that this world gets to know that we were here, and worth way more than what we were given.

To My Seeds

I never meant to be distant, I wanted to be a father in every way possible. I wanted to be there for all of the ups and downs of your lives, but life had a different plan. I hope and pray that all of you are doing well, I hope life is teaching you things to keep you away from places like this.

I can't remember a day when I have not thought about my children, and that's because it has never happened. I want you all to know that I miss and love each and every one of you, and being away from you haunts me in ways you can not imagine. It's crazy how King Leonard doesn't even know I exist.

When you look in the mirror you probably wondered who's looks was looking back at you, well, I am your biological, I wanted to be around but was robbed of the chance.

To all of my children: Lazino, Waykeem, Logan, Symphany, King, Lyric, and Seven, do me a favor, don't believe what people may say about me, if y'all have questions, ask me. After all, I am your dad, don't let othet people speak for you, or influence you to be less than what you are. Y'all are future Kings, and Queens, and don't forget it.

As far as me, I will fight with every breath that I have to get back to y'all, and trust me when I say, I have something in the works. The thoughts of y'all drives me to go super hard, the hardest I have ever went for anything. I will not give up on you like I wont give up on the fight for justice. DNA don't lie, and if y'all are anything like me, you will be talented, go hard, and when we do see each other, I'll be prouder than I already am.

PREFACE

You only live once, as far as we know, so live your life to the fullest. Experience all that you can and do your best to avoid all the pitfalls that will be put before you. Always remember that you are your biggest fan, critic, and enemy. And if you don't love you, whom will. You have to make yourself happy before you expect anyone else to. Love you first, so that you can love others, and remember that God blew breath into you, so let your breath be guided by truth, honesty and love. No matter where you go, there you are.

TABLE OF CONTENTS

INTRODUCTION

It's not often that I get to reach as many people as I am sure that this book possibly could, so let me try to make these words as impactful as they should be. I have been incarcerated since 2016 for a crime that I did not commit. I was sentenced to Life plus 13 and a half to 27 years for a murder that I had nothing to do with. I did not even know the person that was killed.

In my case there was overwhelming evidence that proved my innocence, the main thing that proved it was DNA. A lot of people know about DNA for paternity, but DNA is also used to prove guilt or innocence. I was excluded from everything that had DNA on it. In my case that was the gun, the man, and his phone. There was someone's DNA on these pieces of evidence, but it was not mine. That is just the tip of this ice burg. The problem is not that DNA can't be trusted, it's more that the system can't.

The system is flawed. To be in prison is bad, and for someone who is innocent it is worse. The pain that I feel on a day to day basis can **not** be explained through a book in the way that it actually feels. I can't explain how this experience is killing me, but I decided to let the evidence speak for me.

These are works that I did before, during and after the pandemic. Art, thoughts and poems. I was trapped in a cell most days for 24 hours. I left the pandemic with diabetes and pain from people that I know passing and me never getting to say goodbye. We all go through crazy things in our life, I just want to give you a perspective from a person on this side. We are not all pieces of trash, even though people may treat us that way...and I understand in some cases.

I didn't have proper references when I was creating a lot of this art, I might have had a little picture and went off that. When I was on the street I was a tattoo/peircer, but I used stencils, I never drew anything. But now I draw and paint like I have been doing it for years. GOD is good. I just hope you like the experience that I am trying to give you by letting you journey through my journey. Thank you for your time, I hope you like it.

PEOPLE LIE, BUT EVIDENCE CAN'T

If I murdered that man, the DNA would say that Rodney did it, but instead it says the opposite.

15-0290 – Cell phone

5-0290-1

ĪR Summary: Partial STR DNA profile consistent with Thomas Childs

ne sample identified as EX15-0290-1 produced an STR DNA profile at five of the twenty-four loci analyzed. This STR DNA profile is consistent with a single contributor.

- For the five loci that produced results, eight of the eight alleles detected (Amelogenin:X,Y; D16S539:13; D18S51:17; TH01:6,9.3; and D8S1179:10,13) are consistent with eight of the nine comparable alleles of "K1". Hence, although Thomas Childs cannot be excluded as the source of this sample there are too few alleles to be conclusive.

  - At one locus, one allele consistent with Thomas Childs was not detected (D18S51:15). Due to the low quantity of DNA in the sample, this phenomenon should not be regarded as discrepant or exclusionary.

  - *Statistical Interpretation:* No statistical interpretation was performed on this sample, based on the assumption that there is no probative value to such a calculation. A statistical interpretation can be performed upon request.

- For the five loci that produced results, the STR DNA profile is inconsistent with that of EX17-0015-1. Hence, Rodney Sheldon can be excluded as the source of this sample.

4

Item 16-0021.7 – Pants

EX16-0021.7-1

Summary: Partial STR DNA profile consistent with a mixture of possibly Thomas Childs and an unknown contributor (designated as "Unknown Individual #1"); Rodney Sheldon excluded

The sample identified as EX16-0021.7-1 produced an STR DNA profile at sixteen of the twenty-four loci analyzed. This STR DNA profile is consistent with a mixture of at least two people:

- **Contributor #1: Possibly Thomas Childs**
  - For the sixteen loci that produced results, twenty-five of the thirty-four alleles detected (Amelogenin:X,Y; D3S1358:16,17; D1S1656:16,19.3; D2S441:11,14; D16S539:13; D18S51:15,17; TH01:6,9.3; vWA:14,19; D21S11:27; D7S820:10,11; D5S818:11; D8S1179:10,13; D12S391:19,21; and FGA:19,21) are consistent with twenty-five of the twenty-nine comparable alleles of "K1". Hence, although Thomas Childs cannot be excluded as the source of this sample, there are too few alleles to be conclusive.
  - At two loci, four alleles consistent with Thomas Childs were not detected (D10S1248:14,15 and D19S433:13,14). Due to the low quantity of DNA in the sample and the number of contributors, this phenomenon should not be regarded as discrepant or exclusionary.
  - *Statistical Interpretation:* No statistical interpretation was performed on this sample, based on the assumption that there is no probative value to such a calculation. A statistical interpretation can be performed upon request.
  - For the sixteen loci that produced results, the STR DNA profile is inconsistent with that of EX17-0015-1. Hence, Rodney Sheldon can be excluded as contributor #1 in this sample.
- **Contributor #2: "Unknown Individual #1"**
  - For the sixteen loci that produced results, nine of the thirty-four alleles detected (D3S1358:15.2, D10S1248:16,17; D16S539:12,14; D18S51:12; D8S1179:12; D19S433:15; and FGA:21.3) are inconsistent with the alleles of "K1" and EX17-0015-1. Hence, Thomas Childs and Rodney Sheldon can be excluded as the source of these alleles. For the purposes of this report, the source of this profile shall be referred to as "Unknown Individual #1".

Item 15-0289.1 – Pistol

EX15-0289.1-1 (grips)

STR Summary: Partial STR DNA profile consistent with an unknown male (designated "Unknown Male #1"); Thomas Childs and Rodney Sheldon excluded

The sample identified as EX15-0289.1-1 produced an STR DNA profile at seven of the twenty-four loci analyzed. This STR DNA profile is consistent with a single contributor.

- The STR DNA profile is inconsistent with those of "K1" and EX17-0015-1. Hence, Thomas Childs and Rodney Sheldon can be excluded as the source of this sample.
- The STR DNA profile contains Amelogenin types of X and Y, indicating that the source is male. For the purposes of this report, the source of this profile shall be referred to as "Unknown Male #1".

EX15-0289.1-2 (trigger)

STR Summary: Partial STR DNA profile consistent with an unknown male (designated "Unknown Male #2"); Thomas Childs and Rodney Sheldon excluded

The sample identified as EX15-0289.1-2 produced an STR DNA profile at six of the twenty-four loci analyzed. This STR DNA profile is consistent with a single contributor.

- The STR DNA profile is inconsistent with those of "K1" and EX17-0015-1. Hence, Thomas Childs and Rodney Sheldon can be excluded as the source of this sample.

DADDY'S AWAY

"BUT HE LOVES YOU"

WRITTEN BY

RODNEY SHELTON

I don't pretend to be perfect
Because **no one** on this earth is.
Not the person who put handcuffs on my hands,
And not a single judge on the stand.
I know that you miss me, I want you to know that I miss you too.
I pray to God that you don't repeat all the things I had to go through.
The most important things in life are worth fighting for. So I will fight for my freedom so I can fight for you.

Some fights are not fought with hands, some are fought with words.
Some fights require books, because to fight you have

6

to learn.

I want you to remember that you are worth so much more than the world will show, and when you discover who you are, "the world will know."

I want to give you so much more then just a card in the mail, or words on a phone. Some things I can teach you even though I'm not home.

I want you to know your worth, finish school because what you learn will help you in the future.

Chase your dreams, because if you believe it you can achieve it.

There is nothing new under the sun, life is what you make it.

Your life belongs to you, do your best and don't waste it.

Please don't follow the crowd, set your own trends, create your own style, always think big.

Always remember its hard for mom to have to raise you alone, she loves you that's why she cant just leave you alone.

If something doesn't seem right, stay away it could be danger, trust yourself and your mom, never trust in a stranger.

The world isn't all bad but there are people with problems, there are people who want to hurt you, they will be jealous and rob you.
I only tell you these things because I'm not around to protect you, even though I am away I will never neglect you. I will love you when you make mistakes but don't make it a habit, because bad energy brings more bad energy, like a magnet.

No matter how far life takes you I will never be distant, your on my mind everyday your my reason for living.
I love you when your mad, I love you when your sad, I might not be there in person, but I wish that I can. One day I will see you again, outside of these walls, but until that day, remember, its not your fault that I'm gone.

We all mistakes, mines is not being home when you need me the most, but your never alone. Your always in my heart so I will stay on the phone, to let you know that your loved until the day I get home.

Always remember
I love you

WELCOME

Welcome to the D.O.C., this ain't a place where you want to be, so please don't come in care free like this life is sweet.

Some of these men cop a plea to live rent free, others killed people they loved earning first degree.

Feel free to live life, but nothings guaranteed, it ain't fun living in bathrooms eating Chi-Chi's.

The shit that I have seen, would make ya head pop, you couldn't see this type of shit watching Tik Tok.

People walking round with shower shoes and tear drops, jail house tattoos, lifting heavy weights in tank tops.

For some people this is a stop until parole call, to other people this is home for the long haul.

Lifers walk around stressed, I know that I do, talking on the phone to a woman who don't love you.

Putting in appeals and getting turned down, courts

treat everybody like a damn clown.

Child molesters tryna hide like they good men, C.O.s
tell their secrets, and tell us they hate them.

But if you try to run down on them their going to
tell, and have you in the hole, privileges withheld.

What you know about 30 years behind bars, whole
family gone, all ya friends have died off. All he know
is cell bars, desk and 3 walls.

No mail comes for you, money dried up, 30 years to
your minimum alongside bums, who don't ever read
a book or try to study law, they content with the
100 years that their forced to walk off.

Xspeirience17

APPRECIATION

You don't appreciate me.
So why would I waste my time on you.
These calls cost currency, why should I spend my
cash for you to worry me.
Knowing we have nothing in common personally.
We share 7, and that really hurts to me.

You are low class, I used to be attracted to trash.
That's when I used to lower my standards because I
saw a fat ass.
I can't really say attracted, that line was a lie.
I never wanted a relationship because you weren't
my type.

The sex was ok and I was running from something,
and because of my loyalty I turned nothing to
something.
I hate the fact that I was looking past 2 dozen of
flaws. Everybody was saying no, but I was ignoring
them all.

Now I regret each moment spent, because I lowered myself. I laid down with a drug that was bad for my health.

Now I'm down and out, and you can't even help. Always talking bout what you do but you only do for yourself.

You're a project chick, I should have been out of your reach. I ignored the hard feet and the gap in the teeth.

You always asking me for money, when you should be giving money to me, because no matter what I do, you don't appreciate me.

You want a mansion and a ring you better settle for less, there are some dumb dudes out there that can handle your mess, **"not me,"** even in prison I know my worth.

I can't bow down to a hoe, I vow to put me first.

Xspeirience 21

13

BLOOD AIN'T THICK AS IT SHOULD BE

You can pick your friends but not your family.
Life is a lesson but you choose who you plan to be.
I see now dealing with y'all cause insanity.
You was jealous, wanted what I earned, a fan of me.

How sad, because I lost all the love I had.
Using my social while I'm bagged trying to get at a
bag.
Ain't give me nothing when you came up, selfish ass.
And now you want me to believe that you got my
back...NAWWWW!

I trust no one when it comes to funds.
Playing the game with my name, ain't no home
runs.
You want to use my downfall to boost your income.
I'm a daddy, grown man, I ain't your step son.
Stupid trick, even family can't get a pass.

Blood thicker than water, but how you so trash.

I know some of y'all glad that I'm gone, it ain't really surprising,

I should have known you would cross me, why did I trust a liar.

Xspeirience19

FIRST THOUGHT

When you woke up this morning, what was the first
thing that came to your mind?
I hope it was something like, this is going to be a
great day to let the inner me shine.
A great day to say you love them, forgive the petty
transgressions.
If their good outweighs their bads, let it go for
blessings.
Life is way too short to hold on to the past, you have
a future to conquer, turn that frown to a laugh.
Let your hurt be a teacher, let that pain be a guide.
Now you know who to trust, you are no longer blind.
This is a great day to grow, let the light be your
crown.
Don't wait until tomorrow, try doing it now.
It's a great day to learn, push yourself to the limit.
If it's knowledge inside that book, read every page
until finished.
It's a good day to work out, it's a good day for a
change.

It's a great day to be breathing, a great day to give praise.

Tomorrow is never a sure thing, so while all is ok, be thankful and take full advantage of this day.

Xspeirience 21

Jay

GETTING OLD

AIN'T THAT BAD

A lot of us knows how it feels to get old, we just
don't want to talk about it.
Less energy, less attention, hair balding,
hypertension. Age is just a part of life, and there are
things I didn't mention.

Your wisdom makes you an asset, and your greys
distinguish your appearance. You have lived through
many storms with ease, some youth see you as
fearless.
You always have the answers, even when they hate
that they have to hear it. But in the end, they know
your'e right, even with glasses you see it clearer.

You've made mistakes, made them again, you've had
practice and it shows. You create ways out of
nothing, you turn pay checks into homes.
Nobody lives forever, one day we will all be gone. You

keep making your mark no matter where your'e at,
and watch your legacy live on.

Them young people will talk trash, they should be
proud to reach your age. You came too far to give
up, a lot of people you knew are incarcerated or in
the grave.

Every wrinkle shows strength, power and wisdom.
You're here because you were meant to be, you
heard God and you listened.

Don't be ashamed to get older, just live your life to
the fullest. Take care of your body, you could be
dodgeing a bullet.

Do the best with what you have, if you want to
change it, why not.

Whatever you do be wise about it, even when they
are not.

You have to lead by example, let your experience
shine, they will think with their privates, you'll be
using your mind.

When them young one's get older, and responsibility
comes. I hope they learned from their elders, instead

of rappers and bums. I hope they have them
employment, a car and a place, and when they
think of good examples, I hope they visualize your
face.

Xspeirience 23

GO HARD

GO HARD, don't hold back, life's too short for all that.
NO, is just a word, don't let it stop your success.
You have to push to reach your goals, always remember, you're blessed.
Your'e blessed to be alive, that means you still have a chance.
You can change someones life for the better, be that hero in advance.
Sometimes to change your way of life, you have to change your way of thinking.
You can let go of that addiction, that's the cause of your affliction.
Aspire to go higher, speak your dreams to life.
Call on the higher power you believe in, let God have your fights.
We all have something we want, sometimes we neglect our real needs.
We confuse hate with love, sex with love, and survival with greed.

Life is what we want it to be, but time is not on our side.
If you waste what is not yours to give, you'll be shorted every time.
So please, think before you make your moves, treat everything like chess.
Except when you see someone in need, don't neglect them like the rest.
Karma might not be real to all, but some believe it's true.
Because the way that it goes out is not always the way it comes back to you.
GO HARD

Xspeirience23

Is This Punishment

I don't know what keeps me in the fight, maybe it's the voices of my children...that I don't get to hear much, but when I do, it does make a difference.
For a little while.
Just a little smile from a female that I could see myself with, would make me feel like I am truly worth something.
But I have not felt that kind of love in a very long time.
When I dive in my mind searching for the good times, it reminds me of the lines I should have said, the feelings I misred. I hate the regrets, my emotions are not in check...I'm a mess.
This has got to be punishment for something. I search all my deeds for relief on why all this misery has come to be. The pain that I feel is unreal, but yet real enough to see.
What's wrong? they ask, but they really don't care. If I was to say what I was feeling, could they help me with that.

Would they even try to be there if I decided I couldn't take it no more. Could they help me with these demons or would they bring me some more.
I can't accomplish any goals, I fall short on every endeavor, my help can barely help, and my strength is losing leverage.
I'm tired of praying for things that seem like they will never manifest, the prison life is killing me, I'm saturated in stress.

Xspeirience 19

Kevin

MENTAL

I need a mental health day, because I'm losing my
grip on reality.
It's important to realize that we're just flesh and
bones, sometimes I don't know how to be.
Or who to be.
It's ok to have to free your mind, It's ok to feel
upset.
Sometimes you just don't want to hear, it will be
alright or, today's just not your day.
Today might be a continuation of a bad week, A bad
month.
Why front.
You might not be feeling life right now, you might be
mad at you wife right now.
Your husband might have messed up and took your
life force down.
Your will to live is low, your money's moving slow,
your kids won't listen, your plants won't grow.
Every corner you turn, there's another problem,
another situation, with no way to solve it.

I just need a day to chill, a day to free myself from the drama, peace is instrumental for my mental.

So I take a deep breath.

Breathe in, Breathe out.

Things could be worse, somebody passed last night and couldn't afford a hearse.

Somebody's child is in a bad foster home, somebody's strung out on the perks.

Somebody's paralyzed from the neck down, and won't ever get to have sex.

Somebody has been blind since birth, and can't witness the sun as it sets.

I think about these things a lot, because those could be our fate.

There is always someone doing worse then you, compared to them, you're doing great.

KEEP YOUR HEAD UP, LOVE YOURSELF, BECAUSE IF YOU DON'T, NOBODY WILL.

Xspeirience23

PERSON IN THE MIRROR

When you look in the mirror, what do you see?

The person you are, or who you could be.

This has nothing to do with your family tree.

And you don't need to enlist to be all you can be.

Success, it's just a word until you believe that it's more.

You'll know when you've arrived, just walk through the door.

Don't speak death on your quest, speak **you** winning to life.

Stay away from the drama, put the anger on strike.

I don't care if you're gay, straight, skinny or fat.

Love the person you are, and they'll love you back.

We all have a problem, there is no one that's perfect.

We all struggle with something, everyone of us hurting.

When you fall just get up, dust off your attire.

Get back on your grind, never stop, stay inspired.

You got this, **say it loud**, deep down you know.
Because that person looking back in the mirror said
so.

Xspeirience 18

WHAT IS PERFECT?

Practice makes better, but it can never make
perfect.
You may look at that person as their flawless, but
some opinions are worthless.
44 years on this earth, and I have never seen a
faultless person.
You may not have all that they have, but that
doesn't mean that you're worthless.
Perfection is just a word, that's all it will ever be.
We are humans, so being unblimished is something
we will never see.
Just be yourself, that's good enough, life is a bunch
of lessons.
You may never see the best of life, but be thankful
for your blessings.
A nickle is mint condition when it's fresh out the
mint.
But even when it has knicks and scrapes all upon it,
it's still worth 5 cent.

Just strive for excellence, though you might not reach it.
Nothing is absolute, but stretch, with high hopes that one day you'll acheive it.

Xspeirience23

THE QUEEN

When I think of strong black women, there are
plenty that cross my mind.
But there is only one in particular that sets the mold
over time. That mold is now broken, there will never
be another.
Like the **Queen** that I know, I'm proud to call you
grandmother.

Phenomenal woman, you are the root to our family.
The last big mamma, you bought that view to
reality.
My Memories are vibrant with visions of your
strength. Leaving the baseball field after work, to
come home and cook us some fish.

I still remember the first time I saw you, at 725
Potter. Jherri curl in your hair, in your arms a
chihauhau. A big smile on your face, filled with
wisdom and grace.

With a kindness that transcends, **and can not be replaced**. Like the look on your face, when we would be playing in church.

You would turn around with narrow eyes, and your lips would be pursed.

You are the source of perfection, you made unity a vision. The last time I seen all my cousins together, was in that family picture.

That hung for years on your wall, In the middle was you. Who holds our tribe together, your the last drop of glue.

There's a lot of Meltons and Bakers, but they're just a fraction of you. They can't walk in your shoes, and they can't do what you do.

You took care of your children, and your childrens, children. You raised grands like your own, your guidance is worth millions.

You always had when we needed, on my face there's a smile. Thinking about all those stocked items, and sodas up in a pile.

Miss *Queen Ester Baker*, there is so much I can say. Your good outweighs the bad, God made you that way.

From the fellowship breakfast, to Wal-mart round the way. Without you there is no us, and you deserve all the praise.

HAPPY 90th BIRTHDAY GRANDMOM

I LOVE YOU

Xspeirience23

"You "

<u>Another</u> day, another opportunity.

Another shot at a better life.

You can conquer any fear that oppresses you, if you let go of the fright.

Of course they'll say you can't make it, their affraid of your growth.

You're just increasing your worth, they swear you're doing the most.

You were born for this journey, the trip is yours and yours only.

Your faith is there all the time, so you could never be lonely.

Stop doubting yourself, you have to push for progression.

They say your disability will stop you, but use that as a weapon.

You heard them say that you're weired, but what's the definition of normal.

To be the same as the masses, will never do anything for you.

Be your authentic self, don't let influences change you.

Let your experiences enhance you, don't let the world rearrange you.

Be that light in the dark, lead the way with a passion.

Help those people in need, when their to prideful to ask you.

You can make things change, you can bring hope to the hopeless.

Your the captain of this ship, buckle up and stay focused.

Xspeirience23

Marley

BEST SEX I EVER HAD

PART 1

Your man will never know you like I do, no matter
how hard he tries.
I made love to your body, never neglected your
mind.
I thought you were mine.
But I learned everything is temporary like the
orgasms we touch, we never used clothes when we
relaxed we just swam in the lust.
You would put your face in the pillow as I drove in
your essence. I call and you cum, I'm knee deep in
your presence.
Phone sex and physical, anytime and anywhere.
No resting...tongue travel from your pussy to your
chest, I love what you're blessed with.
French kissing you for breakfast, you work wonders
with your wet lips, 3 hour long love sessions,
consume you like oppression.
I love being your slave, as you ride me like you're

surfing on waves. I hate when you disengage, but the view keeps me tame.

You're never mediocre, your back curved as I pull your shoulders. I grab your hair and pull you up to caress and hold you.

My hands cup your breast, the sweat lubricates your nipples. I rub them gently, as you move your hips, you make entry so simple.

Your body is a maze, entrance is in between your legs, you love punishment and pain, I love when you misbehave.

Your ocean turns my bed spreads into water beds, little man in the boat, saliva all on his head.

You cum harder when I nail your body to the bed, then suck your spot till you explode your emotions all through the air.

You say I make you give the greatest head, because I take your body places it ain't never been.

I melt hard into your person every time we chill, so familiar with your body, I make you cum at will.

We're eye to eye as we lay, connecting in so many

ways. You use your thighs and pretty foot as tools caressing my leg.

Tender kisses got you reminiscent of 15 minutes ago, you say that you want more and you want it real slow.

You're the one, any demand you have, how can I be mad, when this is undoubtedly the best sex that I ever had.

Xspeirience 22

BETTER OFF

I almost lost sight of who I was,
because instead of loving me, i looked to you for it.

Forgetting my predicament, why would somebody
care about me.

I am a convict, incarcerated for whatever: that
makes me worth nothing to you.
Or maybe it's because that square ass clown can
always do something with you.

"Longer than 15 minutes,"
But that's all I have to give.
I ain't worth nothing to you and honestly,
"I understand."

Because if I was on the streets, I wouldn't be
sweating old news. You're going to always be you,
you couldn't walk in my shoes.

Your man can have you, I don't walk with no leash.

I roam free, I go hard, anywhere that I be.

You can never be my only, because I will never be satisfied.

A relationship with me is a lifetime of lies, a life time of women, I got too much pride, being a hoe all the time is in my blood line.

That's what I tell myself

So yeah

Don't answer my calls, don't send me no pics. Don't write me no letters, my love don't exist.

I'm just fishing for something, but I don't give a shit, I'm going to always love pussy, it don't matter the chick.

It don't matter what we had, or where we have been, bout the love that we made, about me fucking your friends.

I don't want no girlfriend, I rather have me a Benz. I want a red range rover, an account full of ends.

Can't no chick fill that void,

"you,"

I don't really enjoy.

Those days are long gone.

I love family, money, success, can't forget clothes,

everything else... And then comes the hoes.

"Cuz bitches ain't shit!"

Their love can be bought,

But being a "g",

That can never be taught.

I live this life, I go to sleep in a cell,

But my cabinet stay full,

I get bread up in jail.

My talent pays bills, that's how I survive, don't no

hoes send me bread, my hustle keeps me alive.

"so fuck all your lies," your weave and your tatts.

The weed that you smoke, "your lifestyle is wak."

You got your freedom... That's cool and all that, but

only time your worth my time

Is when your laid on your back.

So ignore my calls, I don't need you bitch, we don't have to speak, just speak to this dick!

XSPEIRIENCE 21

Martin

CHANGES

6:30, and I'm on this bunk reminiscent, on how at
one point in time we had combined both our visions.

We were so close, "inseparable," love without
conditions, but the time broke that bond, now we
find ourselves distant.

"I never miss it."

All this feeling shit is seasonal,
the love is lost, we're too far gone,
frankly there's no longer a need for you.

No longer do I crave your smell, long for your touch,
I have grown beyond measure, you're no longer
enough.

The memories have gotten boring....not on your part,
it's just I'm no longer that person, that light has
gone dark.

That view was distorted, my heart was extorted, "life is too short," death can't be avoided.

Friends turn into strangers, lovers temperance becomes anger, emotions worn-out and wrinkled, hung out to dry on a hanger.

I can't say that I love you, that's no longer the truth. I'm not as naive as I was when I lived through my youth. To be content with the lies is to crave the abuse. I had to get away from you, I needed time to regroup.

Now when I look in the mirror, all I see are the years, that I gave to the people, who didn't deserve all my tears. They didn't love me for real, I was just temporary, I was a part time lover, I was never primary.

You were raised by wolves, your ignorance customary, relationships are so different that's why results often vary.

I'm no longer love sick, my heart pumps Robitussin, absence did the trick, I'm not wanting for nothing.

I'm not hurting for love, I am immune to rejection, I romance myself, I relieve my erections.

I used to love you for you, but now I love that I changed, why go back to the past, when there is nothing to gain.

Xspeirience21

CRAZY

Every day its the same old shit, same damn jail that I'm forced to live in. Same old people, same nasty food, besides the different struggles there's never nothing new.
Same commissary with the same old snacks, that I really shouldn't be eating, but I can't send the trash back.

I see the same old guards walking the same old tier, and the same scared people with their same old fears.
I'm not afraid to die, because this really ain't living, I rather be in a box, then have to die in this prison.
I gained a lot of weight, the pandemic made it worse, if I died in this place, I would never see a hearse.
Never have my family at my funeral, crying over a verse, mamma saying my eulogy, pulling napkins out her purse.

I wonder where do lifers bodies go when they pass away, probably the same old cemetery, if their body isn't claimed.

Sometimes I pray I get stabbed up...hold up wait, would I even go quick enough, to over come all the pain.

The food gonna kill me anyway, ain't no future in lying, but ain't no future without a fight, ain't no need in me trying.

My life is irrelevant if I don't fight for my freedom, sometimes I want to give up, but my kids really need me.

Or at least I think they do, but it's really hard to tell, I can't tell what their feeling, because all I see is this hell.

Doing life for a crime that I didn't commit, drives me crazy because I'm losing valuable time in this pit!!

"ahhhh"

My chest hurts from all of the stress, but I keep losing focus because my life is a mess.

I got case laws in piles, books stacked by my bed, bowls left unwashed, I'm trying to live in my head.

51

But this sentence wont let me, it keeps on telling me "DIE,"

I see death in the mirror when I look in my eyes.

What was the judge up there thinking when he gave me life, plus 13 to 27, he ain't get things right.

He knew by all the evidence that I ain't take that man's life, but the DA lied on me, lawyer switched sides on me.

I'm lonely and confused asking God "why me."

I was surrounded by whites that wanted me to fry lonely.

Lying up in their papers, hoping nobody save me, suckers stole my safe when I got booked, I ain't have money to pay him.

They gave me a court appointed, you can't beat them or join them, all you can do is sit back and them fuck your ass royally.

Life goes on, but how long will it take, these people want me to fail, they pray to god that I break.

These cowards tell me these lies and look me dead in my face, like I don't notice their sweat or that stupid smirk on their face.

I can't win unless I dig deep inside of myself, and bring the part of me out that puts the pride on the shelf.

The part that goes consistently after power and wealth, and loves me way harder, then I love anyone else.

Xspeirience 21

Do You Care?

He finally killed himself, but who really cares.
You never paid him a visit, you never sent him no
mail.

His mental health didn't matter, his psychologist
failed, never committed a crime but doing life in a
cell.

His life has never been perfect, he always was sad,
sometimes a person can smile, but that doesn't
mean that their glad.

When did the load get too heavy, when did he say
this is it, who could he turn to for comfort in a jail
full of men.

Life is what you make it, that's what some people
say. I try to make it even though I feel this pain
every day.

Light smothered by darkness, am I possessed by a demon, who want's me to die in a cage with strong lust for my freedom.

I don't think the same as I did, time has left in a flash. I just want to go to sleep and wake up in the past...or maybe never wake up, let me ask you a question, if you die in your sleep, do you dream forever.

I'm living a nightmare, haunted by my ambition, because no matter how hard I try, my drive is trapped in a prison.

God don't answer my prayers, I gave up on religion, what's the use of having talent or even drowning in wisdom.

My pain is my pain, my sorrows forever, life sentence on my back saying I will leave this place never. Constant headaches where the pills I take have no affect, can't even masturbate, I'm absent thoughts that get me erect.

Or maybe it's the chemicals that they put in the juices, whatever it is it corroborates my definition of losing.
No control over my own life, led to death by the system, property of the state, being housed in a prison.
Traumatized by the courts on a suicide mission, I'm dyeing rapidly from all of the stress and the tension....
But nobody will listen.

Time makes you irrelevant, words have no meaning when your silence umbrellas your excellence.

I'm lost without a map, my GPS is my struggle, my sons try to be me, but their out shined by my hustle.

I illuminate a room because of my addiction to knowledge, I was gaining hands on experience while you were drinking in college.

So why do I feel hopeless and hope to GOD they don't notice, on the outside I'm a whole piece but on the inside I'm broken.

I'm sorry for my pain, hate and rage got me tired, and not for a nap unless the sleep leaves me expired.

My children become unrecognizable because of my absence, I can't see them oftenly and the time plays a factor.
I've missed all the plays, the parties, PTA's. I was deleted from memories, their minds I can't change. All my days are the same, I'm a number, no name, my life is in shambles but do you care anyway?

Xspeirience 21

Damn

She let me in, I waited so long for this moment, it was more than I expected and worth every second.

Her lips so soft and wet, my dick so hard, erect. Her skin as black as night, she glistens as it flexes.
She rides like an all wheel drive, she never misses a beat, she holds on tight with her thick ass thighs, and her super pretty feet.

She's in my eyes while moaning loud, biting her lip with her teeth, I grip her ass to guide her moves as she releases all her freak.
Her smell Chanel, her hair is real, her nipples hard, I love her feel, nothings concealed.
That makes it better, I kiss her neck, which makes her wetter, her juices flow and wets the bed as she slips and slides up and down my head.
She came again, her body shakes, and I see all the pleasure run through her face.
We switched positions, she face down in the pillow, I

slide inside, she spreads her thighs, I release her tension she loses her mind as I stroke with rhythm.

We collide in lust.

Pushing her to her highest limit is an ultimate must.

I make it my duty to please, I swing more than dick when I'm on my knees.

My tongue in her spot, from the back or on top, it might be cold outside, but when we sex it's so hot.

To the world your so modest, intelligent and so humble, but in the bed your as wild as a beast in the jungle.

I'm honored to be your pick, for all of you I pursue.

There's no limit to the things I won't hesitate to do.

I want you to come, I'm aroused by your faces, I want them back to back, I can't help I'm impatient. I can never be basic when it comes to love making, I venture every part of her body, I desire her naked.

I'm in love with the feeling I get when she screams, then the count bell rings loud...and I'm awoke from my dream.

Xspeirience 21

60

ENVY

Would it be a lie if I was to say that I don't love her.
I know I have love for her, even though its been five
years since I have seen or touched her.

But I am a new person, she don't know me no more.
I'm so far from being a husband, my disease has no
cure.

My drive is fast forward, my ambition is strong, I
have love for some people, for the rest I have none.

Is prison my destruction, is love a game that I play.
I treat women like chess, they are the pawns in my
game.

Ain't no queens on this board, life's too short to lose
focus.
If I give them my heart, I'll regret when it's broken.

I'm addicted to variety, life has bred me that way.

I live no strings attached, I prefer pay to play.

Let's just do what we do, ain't no sleeping together, this ain't love this is lust, both of those words have 4 letters.
Like shit, piss, or hate, that's what I have in my heart.
I don't know when it will stop, I don't even know when it started.

My reach physically is long as my pants, but mentally its extent can reach the lands of Japan.

I'm too versed to be submerged with people who can't even converse.
The old me is gone, the trial was the hearse, judge was the preacher, court was the church.

I'm not a player I'm a killer by the worlds definition, you can google me for lies, but my truth gets no recognition.

I'm a victim to DNA, a product of a prison, enslaved
I gain wisdom setting up goals for my vision.

This times making me smarter, these books cause
division, between me and my past, my futures not
distant.

"It's here," my tears ammunition to shock all of the
doubters, I can care less if they listen.
So no I can't love her because I love me more, I got a
legacy to leave, that's what I am doing this for.

*Rest in peace situationship, I'm going to leave with
more then I came in with.*

Xspierience 21

FOR REAL

It's so crazy how you can be up in prison fighting for your life, while your wife out in the world fucking for some nikes.

If you gonna indulge in crime then you better do it right, it only takes one time to end your muthafuckin life.

What you think this life about, the prison life real, cross the wrong mans path and get stabbed with cold steal.

Lose teeth out your grill, get hooked on the pills, one thing is for sure you can die up in here.

I have seen people come, and seen people go, I have seen smart brothers, and ones super slow.

I have seen people sad because they trusted in a hoe, until the day they found out she the hoods freak show.

Life is too short for all ages, even shorter when they enslave you, watch the company you keep they might fuck around and bang you.

You can't move unless they say, find faith, pray every day, until the day God come back for your soul, and take you away.

This ain't the life I chose, but it's the life I'm living, when I was a little kid I never dreamed I'd be in prison, my first day up state, they threw away all my pictures, two books that I wrote, man this life is non fiction.

I had to get it how I lived, I was broke ass hell, I'm a hustler, so I refuse to let my self fail, on the streets or in jail, I will never change up, anybody try me, I'm a throw my hands up.

This is all real, I walk tall, I don't run from nothing, walk down the tier they asking for favors like I owe them something.

I say no cause if it was me, I wouldn't even try, some people say that were friends, but I know that there lying.

They're only friends when I can do something for them, they kinda like hoes, because I'm quick to ignore them.

I walk past like we never spoke,
stimulus had these dudes up now they super broke,
I'm going super hard, I don't care who knows,
because my heart is getting colder, it's like 50 below.

Xspeirience 21

LOOK BOTH WAYS

Look both ways before you cross me.
Resume book thick, you Mister softee.
I don't need no team to make your body drop.
It's just me and the glock, who gon call the cops.

Man the worlds changing.
Dude wait until he forty just to start banging.
Twice the age of the young bulls that he hang with.
He get shot down in the street and can't no signs
save him.

FROM THE CRADLE TO THE GRAVE
(Favorite line by the way)
I been confronted with the pain, stress the size of a
Hummer but I'm staying in my lane.
They hit me with flagrant fouls trying to get me out
the game, but I got a set shot it will never be the
same.
"Swish"

That's 30 points in the clip, I used to be humble now the devil lies within.

I'm walking through the valley with these tattoos in my skin, shadow of death all around me but I'm still tryna winnnnn.

Major move maker, I don't bow down, never.

I'm like wine cuz every year I just keep getting better.

I seen a lot, all the stress got me tougher than leather.

She say she love my ambition that's why her spot so wet up.

Xspeirience16

HAS TO BE

It has to be right, because if it's not, it's all wrong, there is no half way, there is just get better and move on.

I'm running to win, there is no in between, I have wanted the best since I was a teen.

They don't understand my struggle, they can't see my dreams, I have to push this shit to the point that it hits the big screen.

My legacy depends on it, my kids need a story, something they can relate to, that brings their crown's glory.

Maybe this is my purpose, maybe this is my truth, if so I need reckoning, and I have a life to get to.

They run around saying devil, they put trust on old lies, I don't trust things I can't see, I strive hard to be wise.

If you can read my mind, you would probably hate the title, the words would be out of focus, the language probably broken.

Am I perfect...hell no, I would never say I was, because I know the truth, pain is all in my blood.

I don't think that I'm stupid, but I don't know if I'm smart, because what the world teaches me, is what sets me apart.

I live different for sure, I wake up in a bathroom, I learned a lot from the streets, I learned some shit in the classroom.

But all that I learned don't mean shit if I remain in a prison, this lifestyle is for pigeons, this is just a fraction of living.

I have read cases where people have went home and were guilty, I've seen people be innocent, and get treated real filthy.

I can't trust what the world says, because the world is some liars, they only care about self...tell me if I'm lying.

I don't know why I'm so fucked up, I hate this life with a passion, I miss the piercings of nipples, the tattoos on phat ass's.

I miss the life that I had, I miss the clothes and the cash, I got too much hate in me, and the T.V. makes me sad.

The prison life makes me want freedom, the books take me for trips, around the world once or twice, and then I'm back to this shit. *DAMN*

Xspeirience 22

I HAVE TO LAUGH TO KEEP FROM CRYING

What do you know about serving a life sentence?
A lot can talk about it but they ain't lived it.

Watching time fly by while I barely move, locked
away for something that I ain't do.

Black lives matter but why doesn't mine.

Because I'm doing time, or I didn't die.

I can't begin to track how much I cry, from the
constant stress that clouds my mind.

I never get mail, people always lie, they don't care
that I'm here, they don't care if I die.

I often have thoughts of a peaceful suicide, and how
my dad passed away, and I didn't get to say bye.

XSPEIRIENCE 21

"WHY"

I CAN FEEL THAT... I'm changing, I'm losing my compassion, I am so full of anger.

Who can rehabilitate the innocent who's locked in a cage, judge me for my frustration, condemn me for my rage.

You don't understand my temper, my suppression of pain; I'm at my best everyday when there's nothing to gain.

I laugh when I'm sad, conceal my vulnerability, I try my best to pray and hope that God is hearing me.

I wonder what's the reason, is there a lesson behind this?
Is this pain for my growth, will it sharpen my gifts?

I get older every day; they have stolen my life, unfair trial, biased courts *"the system ain't right."*

This is a no promise zone, I can die any night, have a heart attack, die from stress, get stabbed in a fight.

I guess nobody cares, if they do they don't show it, and the people I knew, they aren't friends and I know it.

I just want my life back, have a chance for my kids, but until that time comes I'll be doing this bid

XSPEIRIENCE 21

IF I GIVE UP

There are times when I really want to say **fuck this life.**
It doesn't really matter if I am innocent... because it seems as though I am the only one who cares.

That makes sense though, because before I ever came to prison did I write the people I knew in there...well I never really had anyone there, because I have never bought myself to take on the problems of too many outsiders in my life.

I can honestly say I am afraid of friends.

Why?
Because they hurt you, and in times of need they desert you. I learned that the hard way, them sticking to the script, that's a hard play.

I don't want to lose, it's really hard to walk in these shoes.

My feelings get bumped and bruised, my emotions have been stored away in wait, for that annual day that they can stream down my face.

I feel that I have no place, my future is dead, I don't understand all these negative thoughts circling in my head.

I haven't seen the outside in so long, of course a person with freedom can tell me to be strong.

They don't live this life, or have to live with this pain, work all day for the state, when there's nothing to gain.

I make 50 bucks in a month, we ain't living the same, bm asking me for money like I'm getting real change.

Man, some of these bitches ain't shit, they can care less bout my life, I don't have no girlfriend, I don't have me a wife.

I'm just a nigga in prison, to them I have no worth, all these ups and downs, why am I on this earth.

My heart races while on the phone, my shirt drenched in the sweat, the day that judge told me **life** is a day I will never forget.

I used to be a horn ball now I can care less bout the sex, I thought I had O.C.D. but I couldn't care less bout the mess.
What is my life becoming, why do I really care less, why do I sit around tired with all this stress on my chest.
Feels like I'm swimming in fire, feels like I'm running on nails, feels like I'm asking for heaven but all they give me is hell.

Should I give up on my life, should I hang in a cell, get stabbed by an inmate who wants a rep in the jail.

I don't know how to give up, I don't know how to quit, I be asking for help, but they ain't giving me shit.

People telling me stories, but I ain't believing that shit, I got a path that's ahead, but I ain't seeing the shit.

If I give up today, I'll be dead in a week, or I might as well be because the pain just wont cease.

But I will be ok, because X is a beast, **I won't ever give up**, until I'm resting in peace.

Xspeirience 21

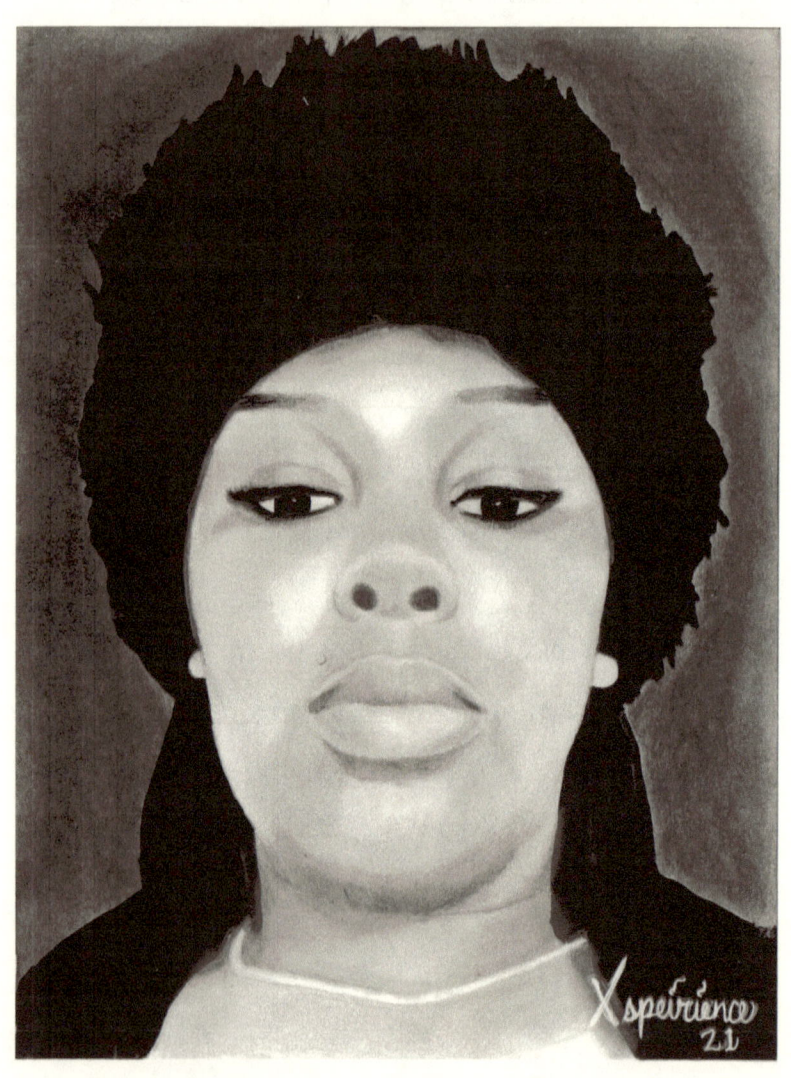

JUST ME

IT HAS TO BE ME.
I THINK... DO OTHERS HAVE THE THOUGHTS I
THINK.

I FIND MY SELF IN TORMENT, BUT I HAVE
LEARNED TO ADDRESS THE PAIN.
IT'S LIKE THE REAL GETS ME NO WHERE, BUT
WITH ACTING I GAIN.

I'm not a fraud am I...
YOUR WHAT EVER YOU WANT TO BE...says the
man in the mirror in front of me, I want to be more
like him, no cares, no tears, THAT JUST MAKES
YOU A WANT TO BE.

THE PERSON I AM BECOMING IS KIND OF SICK IN
THE HEAD, THAT MEANS HE FOUND THAT
SICKNESS IN HERE, AT NIGHT IT LAYS IN HIS BED.

I don't want to be this person, but I really have no choice, I would love to be able to stand up and say something... but I really have no voice.

I'm a dead man walking, I FEEL SO TIRED OF LIFE. I REALLY WANT TO HAVE JUSTICE, but the system ain't right.

I can't depend on my people, because they don't think like me, they can't achieve what I think they can, because they can't see what I see.

MOST OF MY FRIENDS WERE ENEMIES, THEY SAW WORTH AND BEFRIENDED ME, NOT BECAUSE THEY COULD HELP ME GROW, BUT BECAUSE I WAS A MYSTERY.

WOULD HE MAKE IT AT RAPPING, WILL HE GIVE ME A TAT, WILL HIS BUSINESS GROW LARGER, CAN I GET SOME OF THAT.

IT'S NEVER HOW IS HE DOING, could I help him with that, I wonder if he is still breathing, is his health still on track.

THEY COULD CARE LESS BOUT MY LIFE, and even less bout my health, they can't ask me for hand outs, so why help me get wealth.

Want something done you got to do it, can't rely on another, I HAD TO SAY FUCK MOST OF MY FAMILY, even my brother.

Poverty is so real, it turns family to strangers, it turns strangers to friendimies, you have to sort through the dangers.

They never mourn you for long, a couple tears and their finished, they will love you as long as you benefit their goals, and neglect yours for their winnings.

Life is as short as a legless midget, but as long as my sentence.
It's sad when you been down so long you don't mind dying in prison.

No matter where you go, there you are, that should be easy to see, are there other people who think this way, or is it really...JUST ME.

Xsperience 22

"Fuc u crying for"

Fuck what they talking bout, cuz their words mean nothing to a person doing life for any crime, "fuck assumptions."

I walk with the lions, but I am something more fierce, I have explored more land, and have shed more tears.

My experience makes me dangerous and my pain keeps me safe, my heart is a safe, its contents can't be replaced.

I'm addicted to winning, I am what I eat, I grew up in the struggle, now I'm allergic to streets.

I turned fails to successes, made use of my time, I stopped using my pistol and started using my mind.

I had to reroute my grind to find all I was missing, I put time into books and upgraded my wisdom.

I tried to give life to my sons but them boys didn't listen, so they will never indulge in the money I'm getting.

My baby Lyric needs me, because her mom has no clue, I left our past in the past, with the rest of the trash.

My future depends on my hard work, either I lose or I win, I'm a man with ambition, a boss in this skin. How would you face a life sentence, would you cry and give up. Would your family ride, or would they leave your ass stuck.

What makes you happy at night before you rest in your bed, sometimes I think happy thoughts, sometimes I think thoughts of dread.

Sometimes the psychologist I see tries to put me on meds, but that bitch must be trippen, "I think she sick in the head."

I can only be me, being fake is for suckers, they say you only live once, a life, you can't get another.

A lot of people I know are useless like used rubbers, no ambition or drive, they can die any summer.

funeral be so packed like they were doing the most, mamma talking bout her son like he ain't shoot up them folks.

Like he ain't hurt all them families, like he ain't chill with them thugs, like he ain't spend all his money on guns, strippers, and drugs.

He left his children with nothing, he was just living his life, getting shot by his homey, best thing he did in his life......*rip ignorance*

Xspeirience 21

No Choice

I'm about to take you on a ride.
Through the real dark side, where nightmares come
to life all the time. This is deeper than a ryme, this
is full time punishment for crime, you can die in this
place, you could lose you sane mind.
Picture behind enemy lines with some total
strangers, people taking each others stuff walking
around with bangers. You can get raped, took
advantage of cuz you look weak, some one done took
your man hood because you look sweet.
You gotta watch these dudes close because most of
them foul, picture being cell mates with a pedophile.
You got a child you want to kill this nigga, C.O.s
won't let you move you better hide your pictures.
Some dudes want to feel safe so they run to religion,
he great Asalamalakum in his heart he a Christian.
I'm just telling you the truth so you don't make a
mistake, and end up in a prison as a new inmate.

Xspeirience 20

NOT WRITTEN IN STONE

I love my people, but when I seen lil nas x kiss that man on stage, I lost faith in the future, I'm not content with this change.

I have nothing against gays, I just don't like force feeding.

If that's your life by all means, live like you want queeny.

A fake ass and fake tits, a wig and fake lips, doesn't make you a chick, you were born with a di#@.

Be yourself, please don't try to trick a person, some people are offended, they might try to hurt you.

I was raised in the 80s when that life was stigmatized, so it's hard to switch a mans thinking, every-bodies not into guys.

Some youth are confused, hypnotized by agendas,
ain't none of us saints, every one of us sinners.

I don't want to judge people but when it's up in my
face, I can't ignore the dumb shit, I wasn't raised up
that way.

Just cause a man got some lashes and walk around
with a bag, that don't make him a girl, because he
still is a man.

You can be on Ru pauls show, walk around all sash,
put a bra on your chest and a thong in your ass.

Why do a hate crime for dislike, just live by the
truth, I ain't changing for sheep, I don't care what
they do.

I don't hate a man or woman because their different
then me, because we all are humans, and we all have
our thing.

I have kids that I love, and some of the gays do too, they have to live out that life, I have to live out mines too.

I don't hate you for being who you were born to be, I love you as a person, I want you to achieve, I want you to be happy, please follow your dreams, you make this world more brighter, you make people believe.

You can celebrate pride, you can march in the streets, you can moan all loud, you can suck your teeth, you can wear red bottoms, you can have 2 million fans, just love who you are, whether woman or man.

Xspeirience 21

OLD DOGS

Are you for real right now!!!

Talking all this "you this, you that shit," where's all
your awards, who can vouch.

I believe about half of what comes out of your
mouth.

Do I owe you something?
If I do please let me know, because you act like we
related, how did we become bros.

I'm from the old school, I ain't with the new tricks,
music don't influence my moves, and I was born
with a dick.

You might have your youth, but I have this wisdom,
you wasn't shit on the streets, you better off in a
prison.

All that shit you be talking won't effect how I live, you swear to God you a man, but your actions say kid.

Damn young man, I don't know why you want to test me, I can win without trying, you can not get the best me.

I'm official for sure, you can see in my shine, just pray you make it to this age, hope you still got a grind.

When I was your age, I was distracted from goals, I was seduced by trashy people, I was addicted to hoes.

The time made me wiser, the pain made me grow, I'm light years ahead, even when I act like I'm slow.

Quit eye hustling my cabinet, keep watching my moves, you're to snitch like for secrets, you couldn't walk in my shoes.

I'm so confused bout the future, when the youth is this lost, even with technology advances, y'all still drop the ball.

you'll still snitch on your friends, drop a dime on your mom, switch sides on your pops, give fleas to your dog.

Loyalty is out dated to you, that's a well known fact, young people make a lot of mistakes, you don't have to be black.

Some don't care about winning, they will search first for a gat, they will team up with their enemies, they do deals with a rat.

My old ass just stand back, like... what part of the game is that!!!
If I go to where these dudes live...I better be strapped.

Because they might try to rob me, shoot me in the back, scared to face what there scared of, quick to run from their problems, got energy for some bull shit, like they were left with no options.

"NIGGA," you live with your mom, no car, no kids... you still get allowances, you still eat out her fridge.

You almost 30 lil nigga but you act like a teen, you don't search for no job, you ain't chasing no dreams.

You an average ass person, there are a whole lot of _you_, I been a go getter, I can't see your view, you swear you'll be famous, but here is some news, you won't make it real far with that trash attitude.

Xspeirience 22

RAISING THEM OVER THE PHONE

I have to keep money on my phone, because not being able to mold my legacy is stupid... on my part, I'm always faced with difficulties when it comes to relying on others to set up visits for us, but I do try baby.

I would never wish this life on the next man, telling you all will be OK over this phone is not like guiding you by the hand.

It's heartbreaking for those who care, a lot of these inmates can care less about their kids, they rather have sneakers and a big store bag so other inmates stare and think that they are the man.

While your child is being raised by a mother who loves the streets more then she loves her seeds, never following her dreams, too busy following her greed.

This is the typical for most, nothing original, I don't have time to boast, there is no need to brag, if my child is unhappy and following fads.

I hear your voice quiver with the words you deliver, what's wrong baby girl? I can tell your in peril, it hurts me when your hurting, your a big part of my world.

I never asked for this distance, I never wanted a break, I missed your first steps, I miss the smile on your face.

I can hear that you have grown every time that we speak, I try to push you to progress, I want your life to be sweet.

But it's hard to get my point across when your lacking samples, I hope your listening to me when I explain these examples.

I will always love you no matter what anyone says, you are a mini reflection of what I see in myself, you are way much more than what the worlds going to tell you, they will be jealous of your look and what you'll excel to.

You should listen to wisdom, but ignore all the trash, take time to think first and please don't grow up too fast.

Your going to be grown one day, that's when it gets complicated, you'll have problems to face, you'll have bills that need paying.

Right now just learn the most you can, and if your feeling alone, I'll try my best to call often and raise you through the phone.

Xspeirience 21

REFLECTIONS

When you look in the mirror, what do you see, do you ask yourself, how many hearts have I broken? how many lies have I told.

They say the eyes you possess are the doors to your soul, your doors have never been opened, and your heart is hard and so cold.

Your flesh is as soft as a pillow, emotionally you are stone.

When you glance at yourself do you see all the men, everyone was a lover, can't consider them friends.

They dig deep in your flesh and leave their burdens within, then give you dividends so you can go out and spend.

That's all you crave, some clothes and a bag, products for your hair, some thongs for your ass. To catch the next victim who just might walk past, in a nice pair of shoes and a hand full of bags....but you like what you see, you have **no regrets**.

You're young chasing a bag, everything is a check. You don't know what love is, all you love is the bread.

Only skills you possess is sex and some A1 head. 1 million friends on face book, on the gram you're a star, but if they knew you personally they wouldn't like who you are.

Another girl lost, taking advantage of youth, ain't never had a job, struggles you never been through. A high price smut, 2 hours in the mirror and still don't know, "that's just you."

You got desires and we know that you do, in the mirror all day and don't know who's looking at you.

XSPEIRIENCE 21

STOLE MY REMAINING YOUTH

When I look In the mirror.... I don't know who I'm looking at anymore.

"Times have changed," there was a time when I was so proud of what I had achieved, now I just grieve for myself like I'm already dead....How did I end up in this hell, I'm growing old in a cell..... will I make it to see all my kids get older, cause I can't even tell. They stole my remaining youth, now I'm looking at myself with disappointment. I hate my situation, how could I enjoy this.

My kids are getting older, and their dad isn't there. Plenty of men going through this, I'm sure their kids are aware, the kids moms are aware.

My dad died on your birthday, I called you for support, but there was no answer, I ask what is the point.

You don't understand my pain, you laugh at my pinned up frustration, you spend your money at casinos, then ask me for some paper.

I'm doing life in a prison, I have nothing to give, I don't get checks from the government, you can care less how I live.

How can you say that you love me, but treat me like trash, aches and pains in my body, all caught up in my past.

How was my future so bright but now the lights turned out, 5 years in a cage, 5 years silent rage, 5 years of depression that can't fit on a page.

How can I act like I'm happy, when I know that I'm sad, discouraged and angry, was violated..."I'm mad."

My pillow is always to flat, this bed is always too stiff, too often I have headaches, I can't talk to my kids.

Suicide has been thought of, but how would Bubbles grow up, what would Lyric think if her dad ain't around to talk to her with love.

Are my prayers being answered, or is this all that there is, am I fooling myself, thinking that God really cares.

My sex drive is depleting, feel like I'm losing myself, tingling in my arm feels like I'm losing my health.
I feel like death is more closer then it has been in the past, but I rather rest in a box then be alive living bad.

Xspeirience 2021

SAME SH#@,DIFFERENT STATE

You did well for yourself, no more hoods you moved
out.
Don't hear gunshots at night, no more thugs round
your house.
You relocated from the north and found a home
down south.
New job, higher pay, new schools, smaller crowds.

In your mind life is better, you couldn't be more
proud.
Your thoughts aren't diluted because the streets so
loud.
You took yourself out the hood, but the hoods still
around.
Your daughters a teenager, she's into what's in now.

She's looking for acceptance, fell in with the wrong
crowd.
So now its new drugs, and late nights hanging out.
You're trying to build a better life and keep food in

her mouth.
You got sweat on your brow, she got dudes in your house.

You put work in at your job, their putting work in on your couch.
Taking food out your fridge and putting drugs in her mouth.
You left a bad situation, now your daughters acting out.
You're confused and disappointed, can't jeopardize your employment.

You came a long way now, off days you can't enjoy them.
You're talking what she take for granted, she talking what brings her enjoyment.
You bought her car, pay her insurance, lay down rules she just ignore them.
Every time you leave for work the Hennessy gets to pouring.

She worried bout the boys and she failing in school,
she distracted by all the drug dealers and
neighborhood fools.
It's like she want you to lose your job and also lose
your cool.
Throwing lies all in your face like she got something
to prove.

What do you do? Let her get away with her actions?
Or sit her down and have a talk about all that is
happening.
Either way things got to change, how can you
possibly live?
With strangers all around your daughter while
hanging out in your crib.

Xspeirience 21

I was sitting in the day room one day watching the TV, this was before I actually could afford a TV. Anyway, I'm sitting there when these two guys walked past me to this other guy sitting with his head phones on his ears.

The guys were so close to me that I could hear every word that was said at the time, the smallest guy told the guy with the head phones that he better give him his commissary bag or he was going to fuck him up.

What I got from this was that the guy with the radio didn't even know this guy, but this was an extortion attempt. There was a lot said but by the end of the conversation the guy said no and started walking to his cell, the two guys that had just approached him went to a cell on the bottom tier, which I'm guessing was their's, after they were in there a couple of minutes they both walked back out and up to the guys cell who told them no.

It was too far to hear what was being said, but I could see clearly, the two guys ran in the cell and I guess they all were getting into it, a couple minutes later I saw I was wrong because the one guy came out with a shank in his hand that had blood on it, then the other guy came out with the guys commissary bag. The last guy came out holding his chest and his belly, as soon as he came out he passed out on the floor, that's when the guards ran in, about that time the two guys had already made the commissary bag disappear.

They approached the guys after the dude that got stabbed up told them who did it, and that was a couple hours after the stabbing. They locked us all down for a while but everything went back to normal.

The next day I heard that the guys lung had collapsed and he had been stabbed 12 times. Its crazy to think that the guy who got stabbed almost died over $70 worth of snacks, I have seen so many situations where the people actually do die, can you imagine getting killed over yum yums and wam wams, this prison shit is crazy, and if you ever find yourself under the gun you better know how to play chess...not the one on the board, but the one with your life.

AUTHORITY

If you were to ask my opinion on this over see'er situation, I would say... Do they deserve that much power over another mans life. These so called C. O.s are only different because they wear different clothes. A lot of them take this job way too seriously, and should be ashamed of how they treat people. I hate the way that they do things, but I do believe that there is a need for "authority", but to have a person that is younger then me telling me what to do is humiliating to me.

I woke up this morning ready to go to work, which at 7:00 o'clock in the morning is going to get the carts with the trays, some people say that I have a lot of jobs and maybe I do, but all these jobs help me keep my mind off of the BS.

Doing life is one thing, but doing life with the wrong c.o.s makes it worse.

When I first came in this place I was expecting to see the things I had been seeing on T.V. for years. Like going to the cafeteria and everybody basically getting what they wanted, or at least having full portions. I quickly found out that was show biz, nothing more nothing less.

It's a lot about these places that are true like, you can die in here, from old age or from violence, and I have seen a lot of people take their own lives.

There is a lot of homosexuality, the system really does not care about your health or anything else such as mental or physical. You are basically on your own, they have things that they are supposed to have to make everything look official, but that's rarely care.

The staff will call you to make sure that it's documented, but there is no real rehabilitation. I have had a hernia for four years now, and these people know about it. They told me that if it's not looking like it's about to bust out my stomach or red around it, they can't do anything.

I know that these are lies but I have not went back because I would hate to have to curse someone out.

I have extreme pain from it that only started to stop when I started pushing my intestines back in myself, the sound it makes is crazy, and the feeling is even worse.

Your treated like a child most times, you have to move when they say move and be on time with a pass like your in elementary school. It's funny because this morning I got pulled over in traffic by a white shirt, it was like the cops pulling you over on the street, he was like:

"Hey big guy"

"What's up?"

"Come here," (he told the guy that was with me to keep walking).

This bitch ass dude proceeded to ask me questions, he went through my paper work and patted me down. It's crazy because when I looked in his eyes it was like looking at icy blue devil eyes, it seems like a lot of these C.O.s up here have a lot to prove. I don't know if it's because their white or if it's just the area.

Either way, when the violation arises, there are all types of ways you can look at it.

I see it like I'm treated like a kid, I honestly think that's one of the worst things about this whole situation. I hate to be treated like I am less than, I feel like a slave and I have to stay busy to avoid the thoughts that I have on the regular.

I hate this life and I would be lying if I said that I deserve this. I never seen the victim in this case but in pictures, I feel so fucked up because... sometimes I wish that I did kill that man so that I wouldn't be here for nothing.

To be sitting in a cell day and night for a crime I didn't commit is heart breaking, I used to hear that real men don't cry, "shit", don't ever believe that, if you don't cry going through this you are a heartless good for nothing type of person. "I cried in the court room when that judge gave me life".

I'm from the streets but this is way worse than that, you're surrounded by people that you wouldn't be around in your day to day life on the street.

Everybody is not the same but you do run into some of the worst kind of people in this place.

They put you in the cell with any type of person, you don't know what these men have but your expected to put your privates the same place he puts his, (MEANING) you can come in with no diseases and leave out with something. I have no hate for gay men but when you're in here getting hit on by them, it's not a good feeling.

A lot of these guys have nothing but gay things on their mind, all day, everyday. It is crazy because all I do is stay in my cell for the fear of getting too close to some of these individuals, you wouldn't believe it unless you have lived it, and if you can leave this and come back with another state number....? **DAMN**

I want to give you my personal opinion on one of the worst feelings in the world to me. I have never been faced with losing a child, but I came pretty close.

My oldest son was shot 7 times while I was in here, his heart stopped twice while in surgery, I'm a real father so I seen this little guy come out of his mother, no disrespect to fathers who didn't get to witness that, but for me that was a moment I can never and will never forget.

That was a glorious moment in my life, but when that judge told me I had life plus 13 and a half to 27 years, I honestly don't think any moment could top that.

"I was devastated," and what makes it worse is the fact that I am innocent, that wasn't just destroying my life, it was also destroying my children's life, my mothers life, my fathers life.

That is something that I can never stop thinking about, that's something you don't come up saying. "What do you want to be when you grow up?" Locked up...for life, there ain't no coming back from this shit, not in a regular way, this is you got to fight extra hard for your freedom life.

A lot of people on the streets will never have the realization of how devastating this can be, or how the system falsely accuses and convicts people every day of crimes they don't commit.

I can't speak for every body, I can only speak for myself. But the way I figure it, if they did this to me how many other people have they done it to.

I suffer from PTSD because of this experience, no matter how much I try to be happy, "I can't", my children are growing up without me, my mom is getting older to the point it's hard for her to walk. I already lost my father, and because I'm locked up, people took advantage of the situation, (meaning) my aunt took my dads insurance money and didn't give any of my dads family -meaning me and my brother- anything...well she gave my brother $100, she didn't give me shit.

I wasn't looking for anything but my dad gave his body to science, so there was no funeral and there wasn't a casket, there were no real expenses, but when nobody goes at these people, family or not, they think they can get away with it, and in my case **"they did."**

When do you get a break, never when you're in prison, the system wants to fuck you, **and will.** You lose friends faster then anything. They don't care about your situation when it does not benefit them, you learn what life is about fast when you're in this predicament.

Life is short and it's even shorter when your being fed these foods, when your under the stresses that come with this, it's pretty rough.

I wanted to write this book to give awareness of what to watch out for, and to be careful. Understand that a lot of today's world is like sheep, like we have always been but these days false information is so easy to obtain.

A person can spread some news on face book and have all his followers believing every word that he said, then they run to their friends and spread it. After awhile you have the sheep syndrome popping off.

The lie is so deep that nobody knows what to believe, but the ones that do believe it have spread it to a whole bunch of people that think and act like them.

I have had so many cellies who believed what the news and the inmates tell them, "they don't think twice about it." That is what happened in my case, a lot of false information was sent around and eventually it destroyed me, which destroyed my family. I can't explain to you how bad it feels to miss all these birthdays, report cards, growth spurts, funerals, **LIFE**. All I have is my art...and I hope you appreciate that.

French fries, "damn," the things we take for granted, so many things. Sex, attraction, the time with your kids or your wife. When in here, I have nothing I want, so I go for the things I need. I give a lot of respect and props to my mother who is my number 1 girl. I gotta give her what she is owed before she is gone. My mom has always been my rock through the years, if it wasn't for her I would have been given up.

My mom started me out on every major hustle I ever had, when I came in the system I came across an upstate inmate when I was in the county who had told me about people getting there paralegals license while they were locked up. I was in the county at the time and that intrigued me. When I got sent upstate I came across a book that said I could become a paralegal for roughly $1000. My babies mother was talking all this Bull that she was going to get it for me, but like all the things that cums out her mouth, that was trash too. Moms got it for me for real though, she didn't have no real money but she got on a payment plan to make sure that her son had what he needed, and why, because she believes in my innocence, and even better she believes in me.

If it wasn't for that paralegals degree that I got with distinction, I wouldn't be able to even type this up right now, and not because of the skill level but because of the fact I work as a paralegal in the law library. This all came from my mother being the thorough mother she is.

If you can get to your mom, make sure you show her all the love you can, you can run through chicks or dudes in your life, but you only get one mother, and they are worth more than gold when you have a good one.

My mom answers my calls all the time and she tries to do the things I ask of her, she didn't grow up in the computer age, but she tries her best. I hope I make it home to show her how much I appreciate it, how much I appreciate her, because if it wasn't for her, I wouldn't be who I am today. Thank you momma.

You never miss a good thing until it's gone, and in prison everything goes quick. Your body starts to look different, your hair starts to get gray. After awhile you notice people who used to have your back don't answer their phones, or they just stop writing letters. "Its a very crazy situation to find yourself in."

Some people hang it up because they can't deal with the ups and downs of this life, this is not for the faint of heart.

I noticed how this world was as soon as I got here, it's the simple things that can burn you up, imagine using one ply toilet paper when you were used to using

Charmin on the street. That one ply will tear your ass up, "literally."

Sometimes my ass feels like it's on fire when I wipe it, I hate the fact that I have to use this because it's all that I got.

I have went to see the doctors or nurses they have and they tell me I got hemorrhoids, do they really know?

I would think that my opinion can't suffice in this situation because who listens to our 19cent an hour making asses anyway, "we're the slaves," they can care less about our asses burning.

I miss the women but I don't miss the drama, but I guess if it was the drama or this, I would pick the drama any day.

"I hate this life". Even the beds are super different, this shit is like being in some sort of day camp and you just grab a bed because the stay will be very short. They are super thin and as you get older they hurt your body in ways you can't imagine, even if your young they fuck you up.

The pillow is the same, the food is trash and they're always out of something that you may have been wanting bad from commissary.

There is no give with none of this shit, you have to wear your shirt tucked in when walking off the block like a child.

If a person tells you they don't give a damn about going to prison, 9 times out of 10 there lying, and if they aren't lying they have to really be a fucked up individual, or really like being around men and being treated like a child.

"This life can really drain you." Take a lifers advice and don't come to see for yourself.

Rere

YOU NEVER KNOW

These people had the nerve to tell me that I have
diabetes, "Damn," the pandemic fucked me up,
so on top of a hernia and a life sentence, the death
in my future ain't enough.
I guess I'm really walking in my dad shoes now, I
thought I had dodged that bullet, but life had a big
gun, and it wasn't afraid to pull it.
What can you think to take the stress out of the
element of my living, I guess nothing when I'm doing
a long time in a prison.
People on the outside couldn't and don't understand
my stresses, how I'm always a step away from
aggression, how others on the outside use my upsets
for their pleasure.
All the talent in the world can't change my future
unless I decide it can, I try my best to stay focused
but I stay far from short term plans.
Only reason is because they don't work as well as
they should, people say that they can do it thinking
they could, but when it's all said and done, it doesn't

turn out to good...if it happens at all.

I'm used to doing it all, but now when I need things to happen my backs against the wall. I try to ask for some help but they don't move like I move, they can't mimic my drive or even walk in my shoes. What the fu*% am I to do, I hate standing in place, its been 6 years since I've seen my family face to face.

I can't believe these people lied, schemed and gave me a case, now I'm sitting up in this prison feeling so out of place.

The tears have dried, I clean my eyes so there will be no evidence, all the talking to a psych is futile and irrelevant. They go home every day, they don't have to chill in a cell, and sit thinking about their kids, or what they think life could have been.

Lucky me, people lying to my daughter about what my crime was, can't a person on this earth say they seen me line cuz, "hold up, that was my ghetto side."

No one can say they seen me kill that man, DNA won't ever say she seen me kill that man. She don't lie when others do, but she has nothing to prove, how they treat me like I was a loser when I had a lifetime to lose.

My youth is leaving each day that passes, my kids are growing too fast, and every time I turn around another homie is passing.

Life don't come with directions you have to live to the fullest, cause life will pass you so fast like trying to race against a bullet, you gotta get it while you can because time don't stop, just imagine if you were me growing old in a box.

Xsperience 22

THIS STYLE OF POETRY BELOW

THIS LINE IS MORE STREET STYLE,

proceed with caution

_____

Boss

I'm a real O.G., living in captivity, but I stand tall
like the statue of liberty.
I ain't gonna front I been feinding for some
Hennessy, 294, you gotta stab me up to finish me.
Webster dictionary thug, hood but I'm smart too,
loyalty a must, if I said it I'm a follow through.
I'm not a follower so I don't do what another do, I'm
a real boss I'm not content with no IOU's.
I'm used to making moves doing tatts collecting cash,
going shopping with knots fatter then Cardi B ass.
I knew them stick up kids was watching close, Brain
storming, but I kept a clip in the tuck like a news
reporter.
I invest in me so I be protecting me, why call the
cops when you got your own weaponry.
I can't trust another man with my life, I'm a bear
arms quick, that's a humans blood right.

Xspeirience20

BOY PLEASE

All these rappers rich.

Most got the same style.

One clone after another, throw them all in a pile.

Talking about corners that was way before your time.

Telling Lie after Lie doing anything to shine.

"Boy Please."

Your girl known for giving service for the green.

And her pussy is about as dry as an Elaphants knee's.

They say that God blessed me.

I ain't even have to sneeze, these dudes ain't never gonna see me like a home over sea's.

Guess who's a hot topic, with out drugs I'll have your block popping.

I'm not stopping like a high maintenance broad shopping.

Money move like the blade of a helicopter.

22 killed him, when he died he was squeezing a chopper.

Please take a seat

Of course the game got a place for you wanna bee's.

Record lables don't know the real it's just about the cheese.

Say he a monster I agree he got a trap house on Sesame street.

Boy please- stop with all that fairy tale rap

We squeeze, cannons that would put you on your back.

You don't need, dudes at your door with them straps.

Ya girl like who dat, who dat, who who dat dat dat.

Xspeirience20

CAMP HILL, C BLOCK

5:30 they waking me up.

Gotta stand up for count.

It's a lot of people, I don't know the amount.

It's cold as ice outside and it's cold in this cell.

I got this thin blanket, and thin mattress as well.

I'm hearing dudes coughing and sneezing.

Farting and wheezing. All these toilets be flushing,

my celly smoking on something.

When they open the cell we gotta stand in a line.

Then gotta show our I.D.s like it's a license to drive.

Then we walking to breakfast, it's still dark outside.

Gotta eat your's fast. Everythings on time.

Like 3 minute showers, outside for an hour, bed

time is 9 oclock.

People rapping, some just yelling and some be shot.

Cockroaches and mice tryna get in your box.

And ain't no A.C. in this jawn, so when it's hot it's

hot.

Xspeirience18

DEVILS HABITAT

I look out the window and see razor wire.

This ain't a job you can quit from or even retire.

On these shirts the letters say D.O.C and that don't

stand for District of Columbia, oh lucky me.

I'm a convict.

No Akon.

Justice system got me locked up.

A hate crime.

Guilty until proven innocent.

Free room and board.

3 hots and a cot, what your ass complaining for.

Man this, Man this, Man this prison I live in, got me

stressing they tripping.

About these phones they be bitching.

Every 4 days 15 minutes.

Gotta go out when they say it.

Gotta come in when they say it.

I can hear people pissing.

Every sound they be making.

They be messing our mail up incarceration is hell.

Gotta wash out my draws and hang them up in this
cell.

When I wake in the morning.

All I see are these Bars.

I'm so ready to snap but I ain't hanging it up.

Xspeirience19

Ross

I GOTTA LAUGH TO KEEP FROM CRYING PT 2

Everyday It's the same old bid, sleeping in a
bathroom suicide in my head.
I'm so sore in this bed, my back and my head ache,
less then a bean on my books got me mad faced.
Feel like I'm in a rat race, treated like an animal,
thought's eating all at my brain like a cannibal
If you don't have a life sentence, how could you
understand... how my daughters being raised by a
child molesting man.
Face the world, head high gotta stand tall, even
when no letters come and your people don't answer
calls.
Back against the wall, they denying my appeals, all
alone on this road, and I'm rolling on a wheel.
I'm suppose to be hard, S on my chest, like the man
of steel, but I fear dying in prison, I gotta keep it
real.
I moved around too much to have real friends, they
was chasing girlfriends, I was chasing dividends.
I gotta laugh just to keep from crying.

I gotta live but every day I'm dying.

They tell me hold my head... my kneck hurting trying.

They quick to say they love me but I can tell they lying.

Xspeirience19

HUNGER

I'm broke as shit right now, but I'm super rich in
knowledge .
Black Illuminatti and I never been to college.
I'm breaking my mold.
I am the only one.
Fuck what you was told
I do not respect all the rhetoric, tell them to cut the
check.
I'm a man with a goal.
I don't got time for the he better, she better bull
shit.
I do me for a reason.
Life is to short to sit back and not listen, I'm driving
this car I don't care if you get in.
I'm driving right past all you ungrateful bitches.
You can not handle my drive and Ambition.
"Fuck it."
You talking bout what I can't do ain't getting me
nothing.
I am not chassing a hoe I'm not cuffing, I'm chassing

the bread no need for discusion, you say you get
paper, I know that your bluffing.
You act like you tough, but you softer then muffins.
"Really."
You'll get a concussion if I end up smacking you silly.
Run off to go find a gun and come kill me, your
young ass can't fight you just good with 9 millie's.
Your are not rare, people like you aren't prepared,
look at you scared.
You hang around loser's, they targets, they pussy
impaired,
you just ain't making this fair.
Wanna bee's will never be, sweating like it's 100
degrees.
Go get some ball's, and get off your knees, go get
you a job, and earn you some cheese.

Xspeirience19

INEVITABLE

I can't speak for anybody else, but when I need help I
usually got to help myself.
When they know you got life they don't answer
phones, you good as dead, ain't no guarantee your
coming home.
Does my black life matter, am I dark enough, we
was tight when I free now am I worth a fuck.
Where my friends I don't ask because I know the
truth, being loyal ain't really one of your strong
suit's. Jealousy always close, I see him all the time,
but my grind is non stop, ambition sky high.
They want me to die in prison, watch them laugh if
I flatline, they want my kids to suffer so it can
hinder my bloodline.
What can I say, I grow stronger everyday, I'm not
the norm can't compare me to no old cliche's.
Fire in my eyes revenge on my mind, I'm a win, I'll
be back to have you mutha fuckers hating again.

Xspeirience18

142

IT IS, WHAT IT IS.

Some times I wish that I was dead.
Cuz I'd rather be in a casket then living in a cell.
So much fake love.
It's like they pray for me to fail, thinking about
heaven everyday rotting in this hell.
A shell of my old self, this life here is crazy.
Got to maintain while the system openly rape me.
I'm absent in my kids lives, I pray that they don't
hate me.

I'm a victim of racism, a dead man walking, Don't
nobody really listen when they hear me talking.
"Damn"
They took my life and made me look like a
murderer, I'm guilty of some things but killing people
ain't one of them.
Land of the free without evidence makes you a slave,
from the cradle to the grave if your black you
witness pain, at a high rate.
Just stepping out the house is high stakes, stuck in

the hood, we too damn poor to migrate.
Body falling apart, the years just keep on passing,
but a lot of people don't care, cuz they don't have no
compassion.

Xspeirience19

Kim

"LET'S GO"

When you sleep walk through life you could miss a lot, mistakes crashing into you from every blind spot.
When you finally wake up you're in a bad place, with so much baggage you need a suitcase.
There is nothing new under the sun, these kids thinking they're different, but all that you're doing has already been done.
Those skinny jeans that you wear, that was the style in the past, those cowboys used to wear them, but we don't talk about that.
I would like to take you on a trip, lets make a right at the light.
The sign says black Wall street, I know I'm reading it right.
That's the first place I met Karen, that's what we call her today, but in the past on black Wall street we called her Sarah Page.
Same story different page, yeah the struggle is real.
Run in the shoes of Ahmad Aubrey, live the life of Emmit Till.

Both of their mothers felt sorrow, both of them lived with the pain.

They weren't looking for gain, loosing a child ain't a game.

A **white** cop killed your homey, you in the street protesting.

A **black** man kill another, you ain't half that aggressive.

We'll kill our friends for a check, and blow the cash for some clothes.

You'll get your boy a life sentence and hang out with his foes.

These days they call them the Ops, doing drills for some props, you get caught and want freedom,making deals with the cops.

Is that the same as Africans selling slaves to caucasions, "he need bail money mom, none of those prayers going to save him."

Things have always been crazy, it's been in front of our eyes, but now it's cameras every where, the evolutions televised. We gonna still do wrong, and swear to God that we're right.

Our differences are going to cause people to argue and fight.

We are still going to need money, just to live and survive. The sheep are still going to follow trends and spread notorious lies.

We're still going to need shelter, we're going to always need food, we need transportation, clothes, toilets and shoes.

It's so much we really need, I'm not the first one that said it, we need more people in high places, like lawyers and medics.

We need to understand that it's there, that's where we need to be headed.

So lets stop talking about a bunch of nonsense, and go out there and get it.

Written by **Xspeirience**, 2022,
inspired by what I see around me.

NECESSARY

Is that hate necessary, I guess so, cuz I'm a keep

going like Brady, no if, but's, or maybe's

On the streets or on the yard I'm a still be X, you

think you seen it all but really you ain't seen shit yet.

This ain't a movie this is real life, even behind prison

door a brother shine bright.

Leg's long like train tracks these is known facts, my

reputation always in tact and my account stacked.

Ask about me, google got me looking crazy, 19 cent

an hour this is modern day slavery.

Life plus 27 that's what the Commonwealth gave

me, the facts say I'm innocent, but them saltines still

played me.

You can go to school year round with no class room,

eat trash food and go to sleep in a bathroom.

My life is non fiction, it's like I got a pain addiction,

grandmom predicted before 16 I'd have my first

conviction, that or death.

She was right and I ain't proud about it, learned what not to do from the wise guys, ain't no second tries, it's either do or die.
Why lie I fight my demons doing time, I'm from the school of hard knocks, I was enrolled in Jr high.

Xspeirience16

No Choice

I'm about to take you on a ride.
Through the real dark side, where nightmares come
to life all the time. This is deeper than a ryme, this
is full time punishment for crime, you can die in this
place, you could lose you sane mind.
Picture behind enemy lines with some total
strangers, people taking each others stuff walking
around with bangers. You can get raped, took
advantage of cuz you look weak, some one done took
your man hood because you look sweet.
You gotta watch these dudes close because most of
them foul, picture being cell mates with a pedophile.
You got a child you want to kill this nigga, C.O.s
won't let you move you better hide your pictures.
Some dudes want to feel safe so they run to religion,
he great Asalamalakum in his heart he a Christian.
I'm just telling you the truth so you don't make a
mistake, and end up in a prison as a new inmate.

Xspeirience 20

NOTHING BUT TRUTH

My head hurts.
I'm depressed feeling hopeless.
80 pounds overweight, "damn" this stress got me broken.
Sitting in a cell, and I keep thinking suicide.
But I don't have it in me I just strive and endure the ride. Ain't nothing Guaranteed but getting older and death.
But as long as I'm alive I'll be aiming at a check.
O.G. status, just give me my respect.
I'll bust my ass until my death or I don't have nothing left.
On the street I gave them so many bars they was drunk like they had liquor in them.
That hated because I pulled up with the chickens with me.
But in here they just hate because I'm me, I came to prison late 30s, the'll never see what I've seen.

Xspeirience

A NUMBER

Have you ever been locked in a cage, where you piss
and take shit's the same room that you lay.
C.O.s tell you when you gonna eat, where you gonna
sleep, walking around with brown clothes and brown
boots on your feet.
It's dudes who have lost their whole family, they can
never call home.
They upstate stressed out with cancer and gallstones.
40 years and he burnt out, he got a little boyfriend,
they tounge kissing in the yard just ignore them.
The food taste like trash, the water's bad too, bad
health seems to circulate but what you gonna do.
Don't nobody really care that you don't get no
letters, sharing a bathroom with murderer's and sex
offenders.
They don't care if your'e innocent, that ain't there
problem, you got something that they want they
just might try to rob you.
Have you ever woke up with a man beside you, lose a
bet in football now that man inside you.

NL3700.

I'm not a name I'm a number, they say I killed a mutha fucker, only the strong survive, is that true I really wonder, cuz prison life will make you suffer.

Xspeirience20

OTHER SIDE

Damn young bull you ain't even lived life yet.
And now you upstate taking drugs with side effects.
People breathing down your kneck, taking your
commissary.
You ain't nothing without your gun, fight game
ordinary.
All that tough shit don't fly when doing hard time.
People get stabbed 30 times leaving chow line.
Now you turn Muslim for protection you don't eat
swine, the only time you pray is friday when you go
to the Mosque.
If not that I guess you blood or you crip now, tired
of giving up them buns or them chips clown.
You should have got a job and put the loaded smith
down, but now it's too late your boy home dicken
your chick down.
She giving head while you calling she ain't picking
up, and she gon lie when y'all talk cuz she don't give
a fuck.

You on the streets and see these words you better tighten up, they always got a cell and a number for a young buck.

Xspeirience19

Monalisa

To our Sons pt. 2

I gotta stand up for count like a slave, while my son
got a chick name tatted on his face.
Baby momma's want me down, I know they glad
that I'm away, just because I'm confident these
women want me in my grave.
My real friends, I can count them on a hand, day
one's is good enough, ain't no room for no expands.
I changed for the better, my heart is Iceland, I'm in
a place where my career is considered contraband.
I'm surrounded by a thousand rats, racist, retards,
pedophiles and a bunch of fags.
These days they let a child rapist get a pass,
commissarry every week and he eat the whole bag,
what kind of shit is that!
Jesus loves, I hate, life ain't all great. Life is short like
midget legs then you meet your fate. I gotta see a
couple M's before I meet the grave, so all I do is
grind until the time come that I fade away.

Xspeirience20

PICTURES

Your picture perfect, so please don't look at your self different.

Even in prison just go the distance, resistance is nonexistent.

They counted you out, I'm counting you in.

Certified with distinction, I know your destined to win

Fail the first time then do it again, your experience is A1, to curse yourself with failures a sin.

Mutate like corrona and dominate your opponents, just don't stop.

Your the status quo, haters below it.

They be talking about checks but they really in debt, with immature mind sets, that's why they lack the respect.

Don't ask them no questions that you know you'll regret.

Because their as dull as butter knives and you're as sharp as gillette.

Don't give out excuses, you'll have to live with

regrets, and if you give them your time, they need to cut you a check.

Life is too short to be scared, ain't a part of it fair. A person like you is rare, their antics can't compare.

Xspeirience17

YOU NEVER KNOW

These people had the nerve to tell me that I have
diabetes, "Damn," the pandemic fucked me up,
so on top of a hernia and a life sentence, the death
in my future ain't enough.

I guess I'm really walking in my dad shoes now, I
thought I had dodged that bullet, but life had a big
gun, and it wasn't afraid to pull it.

What can you think to take the stress out of the
element of my living, I guess nothing when I'm doing
a long time in a prison.

People on the outside couldn't and don't understand
my stresses, how I'm always a step away from
aggression, how others on the outside use my upsets
for their pleasure.
All the talent in the world can't change my future
unless I decide it can, I try my best to stay focused
but I stay far from short term plans.

Only reason is because they don't work as well as they should, people say that they can do it thinking they could, but when it's all said and done it doesn't turn out to good...if it happens at all.

I'm used to doing it all, but now when I need things to happen my backs against the wall. I try to ask for some help but they don't move like I move, they can't mimic my drive or even walk in my shoes.

What the fu*% am I to do, I hate standing in place, its been 6 years since I've seen my family face to face. I can't believe these people lied, schemed and gave me a case, now I'm sitting up in this prison feeling so out of place.

The tears have dried, I clean my eyes so there will be no evidence, all the talking to a psych is futile and irrelevant. They go home every day, they don't have to chill in a cell and sit thinking about their kids or what they think life could have been.

Lucky me, people lying to my daughter about what my crime was, can't a person on this earth say they seen me line cuz, "hold up that was my ghetto side."

No one can say they seen me kill that man, DNA won't ever say she seen me kill that man. She don't lie when others do, but she has nothing to prove, how they treat me like I was a loser when I had a lifetime to lose.

My youth is leaving each day that passes, my kids are growing too fast, and every time I turn around another homie is passing.

Life don't come with directions you have to live to the fullest, cause life will pass you so fast like trying to race against a bullet, you gotta get it while you can because time don't stop, just imagine if you were me growing old in a box.

Xsperience 22

163

WHY

I had to do this cuz it's the only way you'll hear me,
IM INNOCENT, I hope you hear me clearly
If black lives matter, why am I sitting in a cell, no
visits no mail, because of negative portrayal.
Do you know how it feels to hear a judge say life,
went from the high life to seen as a low life.
I had the perfect job, I didn't have to steal or rob, I
traveled all the time, jewlry because I love to shine.
Now I'm in prison, when by myself I cry, it's day I
want to die, my true feelings I hide because of pride.
I write letter to outside organizations pleading my
case, but nobody really cares it's like they laugh in
your face.
It seems your nobody until somebody kills you, it's
unreal when you're alive they don't hear you.
I could be dying in this place, who would listen,
doing life in a prison is really a death sentence.
What do you know about Chi chi's and commissary?
What do you know homey, whay you really know
homey.

164

Just got a hit from parole till next nevurary

You innocent but found guilty to unfair trials, eating

chow with murderers, rapist and petifiles.

Xspeirience 22

"OK" I know some niggas glad that I'm upstate, so I can't hit their girl's world like an earth quake.

I shine brighter than them clowns on my worst day, catch her by herself and have her dropping it like her birthday.

Loui sneaks with the sweater and the hat to match, kept my prize in some box like some cracker jacks.

On the street I go hard nigga that's a fact, drive through your hood something fly and watch the hoes react, yeah.

I talk heavy cuz I lived this, no matter where I'm at I'm always about my business.

I'm fast forward, life too short to sit and reminisce, I always stay lit, you know why, I'M CONSISTENT.

Gucci frames on my face, check the price tag, I ran circle around them until they waved the white flag.

I been the shit, I been bad, M.J. swag, don't ever think I'm soft I'll black your eyes like an airbag.

XSPEIRIENCE 20

My People

Watching the news, tears stream down my face,

watching my people shot and killed just because of

our race.

Why are you so afraid when you have everything,

over 50 presidents were you, 1 or 2 were me.

It seems to me that you're jealous, but still claim

your superior, we dominate sports but some still say

we're inferior.

DNA was degraded, we gained terrible habits, 400

years in captivity, we were treated like maggots.

Y'all dropped bombs on black wall street, you want

us with nothing, you rather see us in cages getting

arrested for something.

Slave master ain't dissapear, their ancestors are

here, we still wear their last names but they address

us in fear.

They can shoot us in the street, end their shift have

a beer, get aquited like they never did it and thats

their career.

Ain't no justice in this system, I see y'all sleep walking, is Dr. King proud, I don't know just keep on marching.

Xspeirience 20

Johny

STRIPPED

It's 6 in the morning and I don't know what's going on, but it must be something, because they didn't pop my door.

Opportunity for sleep, I can't miss that shot, good movies were on last night, I went to sleep at 1 oclock. I was awoken by sounds off cuffs, it sounds like one teir down, multiple sets I hear now, it must be shake down.

I start cleaning up my cell, I put things out front, so they don't have to search too hard messing everything up. Then thoughts start running through my head...like how did I get here, it never gets any easier, it has been 5 years.

I sleep in a bathroom, this jail is my home, I'm in a 6 by 12 space with everything that I own...this is what life is now, those are the facts, I'm hearing cuffs getting closer, all my loose papers are packed. I.D. and razor, put them both on the ledge, 3 c.o.s open the door, first thing that was said: Take everything off, move your lips, move your ears,

lift your balls, turn around, spread your cheeks,
move your hair, squat and cough, stand back up, put
on your tee shirt and boxers, they put the cuffs on
my wrist and started going through my boxes.
The whole time I feel raped, I can't go any lower,
three men were staring at my privates, my
happiness is stolen.
I can't just shed a tear, right here on the teir, they
got all of us out here handcuffed in the rear.
I'm arrested again, but they don't need a warrant to
search, they're going all through my property, my
feelings are hurt.
I'm a grown ass man but I feel like a kid, subjected
to pain for a crime that I didn't commit, but these
people don't care, they're just doing their job, they
can care less about your feelings, give a fuck bout
your pride. Do what they say, don't resist keep your
emotions inside.
You can't win against the system, so don't even try.
VIOLATED

Xspeirience 21

Random thought's

Four pound feel like 8 pounds when he send them at you.

Choppa left ya car high as mars when he spray them at you.

No matter what I see, I can't say how I feel.

Cuz if I say how I feel it might be too real.

Ya'll the next generation, all shorty got is wet penetration. I'll kill your reputation quick, no hesitation.

I'm so sober, throwing out the trash cuz you wasted, and your so basic, that's why your simple ass love hating.

I know you see greatness, I'm way better then the wine you tastin, my sex been amazing.

I'll take your chick, get her whipped, hit her from the back. It's better if you face it.

xspeirience16

Pussy Cat

I'm in the cell looking at these hot shots I done coped. reminiscent about the thot's I done popped on my tour to the top. Having to sit for this crime got me hot, cuz I'd have shorties running in and out of spot's, knock's resembling the cops.

They got the cuffs and the drugs, so loud neighbors wearing ear plugs, baby I just want to fuck.

No relationships just relations with your pussy and your tits, I'm a dog you can't fix.

I hit never miss, her lips is the target, pussy so fresh they should sell it in the market.

Her head special ed, her four play is retarded, box heating up watch the fire man charge in.

I'm not a player I'm a slayer of them rump shakers, no horse playing, dunk in her like a ball player.

Play the hand that I was dealt like a card player, I got a full house, know how I know, because her walls said it.

I got dreams of fucking a rapping ass bitch lips wrapped around Cardi Bs nips, I got her legs in the air, knees like ear muffs, I got her busting off hard while she riding this shot gun

Megan the Stalion, shit, I bet I'd be whilling, have that pussy so wet we gone have to bring towels in, threw this carrot in her mouth slid it out than back in. She put insurance on her ass cause I tore out her back end

Coochie wet and sticky when I minage with Nikki, Knee deep in her pussy while I massage her titties. Fucked her a day in a half cuz I'm allergic to quickys, I sucked the pussy so hard I left the clit with a hicky. Doja cat, pussy was so wet and fat, I killed that cat like 8 times but it kept coming back.

Holes overflowed Juices running down her crack, I took my thumb up out her ass she told me, put that shit back.

I been down for too long All I think about is freak shit, I want some warm wet slip and slide pink shit, I'll take a tall thick Jawn or petit chick, I don't even care just as long as she a freak bitch.

Xspeirience 19

Xspeirience Art

www.ingramcontent.com/pod-product-compliance
Lightning Source LLC
Chambersburg PA
CBHW021101130626
46554CB00002B/481